New Nelson Handwriting

Cursive Copymasters

Thomas Nelson and Sons Ltd
Nelson House Mayfield Road
Walton-on-Thames Surrey
KT12 5PL UK

58 Albany Street
Edinburgh
EH1 3QR UK

Nelson Blackie
Wester Cleddens Road
Bishopbriggs
Glasgow
G64 2NZ UK

Thomas Nelson (Hong Kong) Ltd
Toppan Building 10/F
22A Westlands Road
Quarry Bay Hong Kong

Thomas Nelson Australia
102 Dodds Street
South Melbourne
Vic 3205 Australia

Nelson Canada
1120 Birchmount Road
Scarborough Ontario
M1K 5G4 Canada

© **Peter Smith 1993**

First published by Thomas Nelson and Sons Ltd 1993

ISBN 0-17-424064-3
NPN 9 8 7 6 5 4 3 2

Printed in China

Contents

A ready reference guide to the main features of the scheme

1. How *New Nelson Handwriting* is organised

Cursive Copymasters A
- Pencil play and pattern practice
- Lower case letters with exit hooks
- Figures 1–10
- Nursery rhymes for practice

Cursive Copymasters B
- Patterns for pencil control and fluency
- Lower and upper case letters
- Learning the joins
- Practising the joins in letter strings and words
- Figures 1–10 (revised)
- Poems and riddles for practice

Cursive Copymasters 1
- Revision of patterns and joins
- Letter strings for spelling
- Practice through themed words
- Practice through poems and prose
- Practice through non-chronological writing

Pupils' Book 2
- Revision of joins
- Developing quality and fluency in joined writing
- Developing good spelling strategies

Pupils' Book 3
- Revision of joins
- Developing sloping writing
- Introduction of ink writing
- Good spelling strategies

Junior Copymasters
- Additional practice in learning joins and models for sustained writing practice

Pupils' Book 4
- Revision of joins
- Quality and fluency in ink writing
- Shaded writing
- Developing an individual style

New Nelson Handwriting Cursive Copymasters Teacher's Manual
- A supplementary manual for **Cursive Copymasters A**, **B** and **1** which provides guidance on the theory and practice of teaching joined writing at Key Stage 1. Guidance on **Pupils' Books 2**, **3** and **4** and the **Junior Copymasters** may be found in the **New Nelson Handwriting Teacher's Manual**.

2. The lower case alphabet taught in Cursive Copymasters A, B and 1

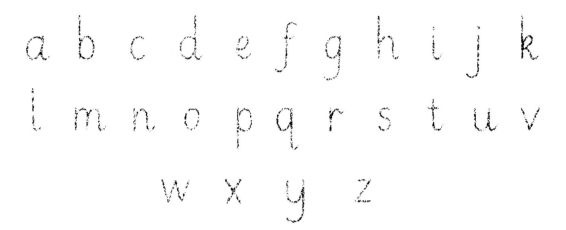

3. The capital letters taught in Cursive Copymasters B and 1

4. The figures taught in Cursive Copymasters A, B and 1

0 1 2 3 4 5 6 7 8 9

5. The join sets taught in Cursive Copymasters B and 1

Set 1   The set of lower case letters which have hooks at the bottom of the 'x' height:

a c d e h i k l m n t u

Set 2   The set of lower case letters which are written commencing at the top of the 'x' height:

a c d e g i j m n o p q

r s u v w x y

Set 3   The set of lower case letters which are written commencing at the top of the ascender:

b f h k l t

Set 4   The set of lower case letters which are concluded at the top of the 'x' height:

f o r v w

Set 5   The set of lower case letters *after* which no join is ever made (break letters):

b g j p q s x y z

No join is ever made *to z* either.

6. The rules for joining

The basic (first) join   The join from any member of Set 1 to any member of Set 2:

in am tu

The second join   The join from any member of Set 1 to any member of Set 3:

ab ck el

The third join   The join from any member of Set 4 to any member of Set 2:

oc rm vo

The fourth join   The join from any member of Set 4 to any member of Set 3:

ob wl rk

The break letters   No join is ever made *after* the break letters. No join is ever made *to z* either.

bigger queen just

pistol boxer zebra yes

Part 1
Basic Principles

1 Introduction

Aim of the Cursive Copymasters

The main aim of the Cursive Copymasters is to provide a joining programme for Key Stage 1 pupils.

In schools where pupils are taught to print at the very beginning, the Cursive Copymasters will introduce them to the joined style at any time in Key Stage 1.

Children who are encouraged to produce joined writing as an immediate development from their emergent writing may need help in clarifying the relationships between letter forms and linking movements, and will also benefit from the Cursive Copymasters.

The Cursive Copymasters will also be useful for pupils who are individually ready to begin to learn a joined hand in schools which do not have a policy for joining at Key Stage 1, or those who need extra practice.

The Cursive Copymasters will ensure that pupils attain Level 3 (Handwriting) by the end of Key Stage 1, *'beginning to produce clear and legible joined up writing'* with *'properly orientated and mainly legible upper and lower case letters'* (Level 2).

Organisation

There are three sets of copymasters (A, B and 1) and a Teacher's Manual. They provide an alternative path into *New Nelson Handwriting* so that children who have used the Cursive Copymasters may move smoothly on to Books 2, 3 and 4.

The three sets of copymasters cover the following broad areas:
A Preparation for joining
B The joins
1 Practising the joins

This Teacher's Manual is in two parts. Part 1 describes and explains the basic principles involved in teaching the joins at Key Stage 1. Part 2 gives a page-by-page guide to teaching with the copymasters.

Letter forms and style

The style of writing and the letter forms taught in the Cursive Copymasters are the same as those taught in Pupils' Books A–4, except that exit hooks are introduced from the beginning to facilitate early joining.

The letters concerned are:

a c d e h i k l m n t u

It is important to ensure that pupils do not exaggerate the exit hooks:

a must not become *a*   *u* must not become *u*

See page 2 for details of all the letter forms.

Slope

The examples of writing provided on the copymasters are upright, and it is recommended that pupils are taught to produce writing which is upright or with a slight slope to the right. If a slope is encouraged it should be no more than 6–8°. A backward slope should be discouraged.

Layout

One advantage of copymasters is that pupils can write directly on the sheet. The copymasters follow this pattern:

1 examples, in black line, for observation/discussion
2 further examples, in a grey tint, for pupils to trace over
3 space for further practice, within guidelines

The use of symbols

Symbols are used to help children be as independent as possible when using the copymasters:

 Observe/discuss

 Write

● Start here

→ indicates direction of movement

For letters which involve more than one pencil stroke, the arrows are numbered. The symbols are phased out as the children work through the three sets of copymasters.

Size of writing

Guidelines are provided on the copymasters as follows:

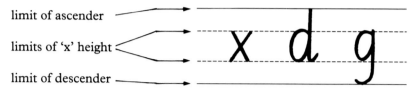

limit of ascender

limits of 'x' height

limit of descender

The size of writing is gradually reduced through the sets of copymasters and, towards the end of Cursive Copymasters 1, pupils are introduced to a policy for writing on conventional lined paper.

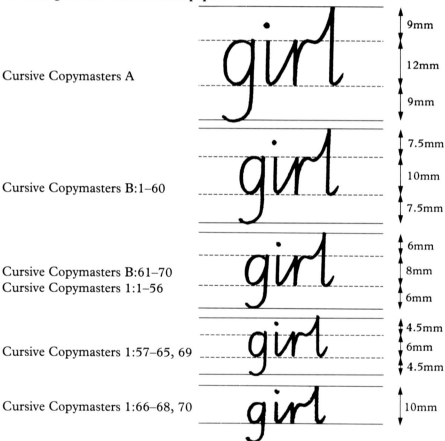

Cursive Copymasters A — 9mm / 12mm / 9mm

Cursive Copymasters B:1–60 — 7.5mm / 10mm / 7.5mm

Cursive Copymasters B:61–70
Cursive Copymasters 1:1–56 — 6mm / 8mm / 6mm

Cursive Copymasters 1:57–65, 69 — 4.5mm / 6mm / 4.5mm

Cursive Copymasters 1:66–68, 70 — 10mm

As they progress through the Cursive Copymasters, some children may prefer to make their writing smaller than the examples provided. If this is the case, they should be encouraged to use the lower dotted line as a baseline for the reduced 'x' height and to make ascenders and descenders in proportion.

2 Teaching method

The role of the teacher

All children need support and encouragement and, as their understanding of the writing process increases and their motor control develops, they also require guidance, demonstration and instruction.

Early Years teachers have an important and sensitive role as they encourage their pupils to write with confidence and at the same time to develop good habits of letter formation that will lead to a legible and fast-flowing hand.

In the early stages it is, perhaps, inevitable that the writing of some children will be uneven in formation, size, spacing and orientation, especially in their free writing. However, the models for observation together with the guided practice provided in the copymasters will help to focus the children's attention on the detail of their writing and lead to improvement in these aspects of the process. It is an important part of the teacher's role to encourage the transfer of this improvement to the children's free writing.

Teaching techniques

As the skill of handwriting is very much a movement process it follows that demonstration is an important teaching technique. Further suggestions for developing readiness and for fostering good rhythmic movement may be found on page 21.

Terminology

During the course of teaching children to write, a variety of specific terms will probably be used to describe letter features and hand movements. Children need to be familiar with these terms and to understand them. Here are some of the most useful ones:

anti-clockwise	diagonal	line	up
ascender	down	lower case/small letter	upper case/capital
circle	downstroke	oval	letter
clockwise	hooks	parallel	upstroke
cursive	horizontal	rhythm	upswing
curved	joined writing	right	vertical
descender	left	straight	

Some of these, together with other relevant terms, are defined in the glossary on page 37.

Posture

It is important to establish good habits of posture as early as possible. Children will be helped by demonstration, illustration and explanation but it is essential that teachers observe their pupils in the process of handwriting and are prepared to intervene with sensitivity when the need arises.

The following aspects of posture are recommended:

- Children should be comfortable and relaxed when writing.
- Table height should allow the forearm to rest lightly on the table, parallel to the table; this allows easy movement of wrist and fingers.
- Chair height should allow the thighs to be horizontal when the feet are flat on the floor.
- The body should be straight, inclined slightly forwards, with upper arms vertical.

Pencil grip

This grip is recommended for right-handers. The pencil should be lightly gripped between the right thumb and adjacent two fingers about 3 cm from the pencil point, while the other two fingers rest on the paper supporting the hand. The left hand should also rest on the paper to move it up as the writing proceeds. The angle formed by the pencil and paper should be about 45°, as should the angle made by the pencil and the body as the pencil points over the right shoulder.

Positioning the paper

Again, this is the policy for right-handers. The paper or page should be positioned in front of the right half of the writer's body and the bottom left-hand corner should be tilted slightly towards the writer.

Helping the left-hander

Left-handers need special consideration as follows:

● Remember that because of our left to right writing system, left-handers have to push the pencil rather than pull it away from the body. Provide a soft pencil with a rounded point. Left-handers should be seated to the left of right-handers if two children are working side by side.

Posture, pencil grip and paper position are similar to those recommended for right-handers. However:

● Encourage left-handers to hold the pencil about 4 cm from the point. This will allow them to see their writing better.
● Left-handers should position the paper in front of the left side of the body with the bottom right-hand corner tilted towards them.
● Left-handers sometimes have difficulty with spacing between words. If they find finger spacing helpful they should place the right index finger on the paper from above rather than below the line.
● Some left-handers may benefit from a slightly higher chair or a cushion as they often try to raise their body to facilitate writing by sitting on the edge of the chair or folding a leg under the body.

Detailed consideration of the needs of left-handers will be found on page 30 of the *New Nelson Handwriting Teacher's Manual*.

3 Writing materials

Writing implements

Before beginning work on the Cursive Copymasters, children will probably
have enjoyed pattern making and drawing with a variety of implements
including chalks, crayons and felt-tip pens. Although these will continue to
be used, standard lead pencils are recommended for use on the copymasters.
Some pupils may need a triangular grip or sleeve to help them attain the
recommended tripod grip, while others may find thicker (jumbo) pencils
more suited to their hands. Some children tend to hold a slim pencil too
tightly, causing tension.

Paper

As well as practising on the copymasters, pupils will write for many other
reasons and should use paper of various sizes, shapes and colours. Much of
this paper may be unlined and the children cannot necessarily be expected to
do free writing on unlined paper with the same degree of control and
regularity as they achieve on the copymasters. Some of the writing will also
be done on conventional lined paper so children may need guidance on
managing this.

(The copymasters include blank sets of guidelines for writing in the various
sizes, including a blueprint for conventional lined paper.)

4 Organisation of teaching

Teaching groups

It is common practice in primary schools for different areas of the curriculum to be delivered to whole classes, groups of children or individuals as appropriate. During Key Stage 1, a group of children may well be considered ready to embark on a formal programme of learning joined writing before others in the class are ready. By the end of Key Stage 1, all, or at least a majority of pupils in a class may be writing a joined hand so that class or large group lessons for revision and further development may be appropriate. (It is also possible that, at any time during Key Stages 1 and 2, individuals may need one-to-one attention.)

Allocation of time

Some teachers like to spend a few minutes every day on the specific teaching of handwriting, while others prefer to spend more time at less frequent intervals. However, there are two stages in the programme when a greater time allocation is recommended, to ensure that correct letter formation is thoroughly established:

● when the twenty-six letter forms are being taught

● when the four joins are being taught

5 Contexts for practice

The main purpose of the Cursive Copymasters is to provide a programme through which pupils at Key Stage 1 will learn to write a joined hand effectively. Many of the copymasters concentrate solely on this objective. However, when practice is required for the taught skills to become automatic and effortless, the writing has been set in the context of meaningful activities in the areas of phonics, spelling, vocabulary development, grammar, genre, and mathematics. The contexts include:

● sound/symbol correspondence
● magic *e*
● contractions
● silent letters
● words grouped thematically
● alphabetical order
● opposites
● verbs
● prose (story and non-chronological) and poetry
● applied figure work

Links with phonics and spelling

Teachers will find many opportunities to introduce or consolidate aspects of phonic knowledge throughout the copymasters. In Cursive Copymasters 1, common letter strings and spellings are systematically introduced. To ensure that the examples are well structured the author has referred to the *Morris-Montessori Word List* [1], which incorporates *Phonics 44*. This is a linguistics-informed system, devised by Joyce Morris, which demonstrates a progression of spelling patterns for teaching and learning the relationships between the 44 speech sounds (phonemes) and the 26 letters (graphemes).

Vocabulary development

In the early copymasters, examples of vocabulary have drawn heavily on *Word for Word* [2] by Dee Reid, which lists the most common words in the written vocabulary of young children. Particularly in Cursive Copymasters 1, where more complex contexts for practice are included, there are specific opportunities for vocabulary development. Read through any unfamiliar words with the children, and discuss meaning and usage.

[1] *Morris-Montessori Word List* (Montessori)
[2] Dee Reid: *Word for Word* (LDA)

6 Assessment

Class/school assessment

Assessment should be at two levels – class/school and individual. At class/school level teachers will want to satisfy themselves that the school policy and programme are effective. A survey of children's writing produced for various purposes allows for a general impressionistic assessment and may indicate a need for detailed investigation. This kind of whole school general assessment is more likely to be carried out if a specified member of staff has responsibility to initiate the process at regular intervals, for example, termly or annually, and then to ensure that any problems identified are followed up. Criteria for this subjective assessment might include the following:

● Is the writing legible and pleasant to look at?
● Are the letters of the correct shapes and proportions?
● Are the joins correctly made?
● Are the spaces between letters, words and lines appropriate?
● Is the writing appropriate in size?
● Is the writing properly aligned?

Individual assessment

At the individual level it is essential that pupils are observed as they write so that significant faults in posture, pencil grip and method of forming and joining letters can be noted. It is not sufficient to assess individual progress solely by looking at a child's finished output although this can be helpful. Criteria for individual assessment might include:

● Does the child adopt a correct posture?
● Does the child hold the pencil correctly?
● Does the child use the correct movements when forming and joining letters?
● Does the child reverse or invert any letters?
● Does the child write fluently and rhythmically?
● Is the writing legible?
● Is the writing produced at an appropriate speed?

A photocopiable checklist is provided on pages 17 and 18 to facilitate more objective assessment and detailed diagnosis of problems. This checklist has been adapted from one in the *New Nelson Handwriting Junior Copymasters*. The author has also referred to a similar checklist which is published in *The Handwriting File* [3] to ensure that this checklist will be as appropriate as

[3] Jean Alston and Jane Taylor : *The Handwriting File* (LDA)

possible. The majority of pupils using the copymasters will make satisfactory progress and only a small minority will require the use of a checklist. However, in such cases, the checklist will help teachers decide on a remedial programme which starts from what the child can do satisfactorily. The checklist then provides for recording the resulting improvement.

Self-assessment

Pupils should gradually be encouraged to look critically at their own written work. Advice is given on some of the copymasters to help children to assess their own handwriting and to repeat a task when necessary. Criteria for self-assessment include:

- Are the letters formed correctly?
- Are the descenders and ascenders in proportion?
- Are the letters and words correctly spaced?
- Are the joins properly made?
- Is the writing the right size?
- Is the writing upright or slightly sloped to the right?

Assessment sheet (1)

Child's name ————————————————————————————————

Date of birth ——————————————— Right/Left-handed ———————————

Tick or date entries to record the child's achievement of each skill.

1. Writing habits
Does the child:

a) sit comfortably and correctly? ☐

b) hold the pencil in an appropriate tripod grip? ☐

c) position the paper correctly? ☐

d) make pencil strokes smoothly and without undue pressure? ☐

2. Basic letter patterns
Can the child make the following patterns rhythmically and easily?

a) *c* pattern　　　　　ccccc ☐

b) spirals　　　　　　　lllll ☐

c) pushes or bridges　mmmm ☐

d) pulls or swings　　uuuuu ☐

e) diagonals　　　　　WWWW ☐

f) straight lines　　　|||–––|||––– ☐

3. Construction of letters
Complete the table below.

a) Are the letters made with the correct movements? ☐

b) Are all the letters except *f i j t x* made without lifting pencil
   from paper? ☐

c) Are downstrokes vertical and parallel or sloping slightly
   to the right? ☐

d) Do *a b c d e g o p q* have oval rather than rounded bodies? ☐

e) Are the letters correct in shape and proportion? ☐

	a	b	c	d	e	f	g	h	i	j	k	l	m	n	o	p	q	r	s	t	u	v	w	x	y	z
a)																										
b)				▓			▓			▓									▓				▓			
c)			▓											▓					▓		▓			▓		
d)				▓	▓	▓	▓	▓	▓	▓	▓			▓		▓	▓	▓	▓	▓	▓	▓	▓	▓	▓	▓
e)																										

New Nelson Handwriting Cursive Copymasters
© Peter Smith 1993

Published by Thomas Nelson & Sons Ltd 1993

Assessment sheet (2)

Child's name _____

Date of birth _____ Right/Left-handed _____

Tick or date entries to record the child's achievement of each skill.

4. Size of writing

a) Is the size of writing appropriate? ☐

b) Are the letters regular in size? ☐

c) Are the relative heights and proportions of the different types of
letter correct? ☐

5. Spacing of letters, words and lines

a) Does the space between letters appear uniform? ☐

b) Is the space between words regular and appropriate? ☐

c) Is the spacing between lines regular and appropriate? ☐

d) Is the writing correctly aligned across the page? ☐

6. Joined writing (Beginning stage)

Can the child do the following:

a) Perform the swings pattern confidently? *UUUUUU* ☐

b) Make the joins correctly and as continuous movements:

the basic join? *un* ☐

the second join? *ab* ☐

the third join? *oc* ☐

the fourth join? *ob* ☐

c) Use the break letters appropriately and with regular spacing? ☐

d) Use the different forms of *s* and *e* appropriately? ☐

7. Joined writing (Mastery stage)

a) Has the size of writing decreased appropriately?

b) Is the writing upright or with a regular slope of not more than 8° to the right? ☐

c) Can the child evaluate his/her writing competently? ☐

d) Is the writing free of the faults listed below?

Letters too short or too tall ☐

Letters with their tails too long or too curly ☐

Badly made joins ☐

Downstrokes not all in the same direction ☐

Cross-strokes of *f* or *t* in the wrong place ☐

Dot of an *i* or *j* missed out or in the wrong place ☐

Wrong spacing between letters, words or lines ☐

Writing not straight across the page ☐

New Nelson Handwriting Cursive Copymasters
© Peter Smith 1993

Published by Thomas Nelson & Sons Ltd 1993

Part 2
Using the
Cursive Copymasters

1 Introduction

- All the copymasters make use of the symbols on page 7, although their use is gradually decreased as the children gain competence.
- Explain the significance of the guidelines (dotted and solid) described on page 8; it is important that children keep 'x' height constant as well as the height of ascender and descender.
- As the letters are learned, they appear on subsequent sheets in a grey tint so the children can trace over them.
- Many of the copymasters include line drawings which may be coloured in.

2 Cursive Copymasters A: Preparation for joining

Introduction

At home, in playgroups, in nursery classes and, perhaps, in previous infant classes the children will have been writing for a variety of purposes and with varying degrees of proficiency. Although it may be safe to assume such previous experience and some guidance it is probably not sensible to assume that any prior instruction has necessarily been consistent. It is, perhaps, more likely that the writing process has been modelled and/or demonstrated by parents and others using a variety of letter forms including capital letters. These copymasters introduce the *New Nelson Handwriting* lower case letters, with exit hooks where appropriate, to prepare the children for learning to join in a consistent and logical way.

Preparation (pre-writing)

There may be some children whose previous writing experience has not been as rich as that described above, and it will be necessary to provide them with pre-writing activities before embarking on the Cursive Copymasters. This section provides some suggestions.

Writing for a purpose

An important task for teachers in connection with children's writing in the early stages is to take positive steps to ensure that the children appreciate the functions of writing. Teachers who make a point of telling their pupils about the writing that they have been doing themselves and about letters and postcards that they have enjoyed receiving are clearly contributing to awareness of the importance of writing. However, it will also be essential to provide opportunities for the children to observe their teacher actually writing. Attention can thus be focused on aspects of the writing process in an unthreatening manner.

Many opportunities to write for the pupils in a purposeful manner occur in a busy nursery or reception classroom. The list would be endless but includes:

- records of collaborative composition
- records of personal experiences dictated by pupils
- captions for classroom friezes or models
- wall stories
- organisational notices
- instructions for games
- thank you letters
- greetings cards
- menus and recipes

Activities to improve motor control

Many experiences commonly provided in nursery and reception classes to foster various aspects of development may also contribute to readiness for handwriting.

Play activities and exercises which develop control of larger muscles include:

throwing, rolling, catching and bouncing balls; skipping; dancing; running and jumping to music; climbing on agility apparatus; hammering; games and play activities involving large arm movements such as pretending to be windmills or the branches of trees in the wind

Activities which exercise the smaller muscles of hand and fingers and develop co-ordination of hand and eye include:

folding paper; cutting out shapes; recognising geometric shapes and fitting them into frames; model making with large plastic Meccano and other constructional toys; building and stacking with bricks; using screw toys and pegboards; modelling with clay, plasticine and other malleable materials; drawing in sand; scribbling and drawing on chalkboards and blackboards with chalk or on large sheets of paper with paint brushes, felt pens or jumbo crayons; playing with tactile letters and jigsaw puzzles; games and miming involving finger and wrist movements

At this time teachers might also:

● give miming exercises to relax muscles:
washing, wringing, rubbing, shaking and folding clothes; brushing hair; stroking a cat; playing a musical instrument; playing with snow, bubbles, feathers, balloons etc; picking up sweets to put in a dish
● give initial guidance towards correct pencil grip and helpful posture

Activities to improve fluency

There are many pre-writing and early writing activities which may benefit children before they embark on Cursive Copymasters A. Some could also be usefully undertaken as extensions of the worksheet activities.

The exercises which follow under separate headings are not intended as a rigid scheme of work which must be followed; teachers should select appropriate tasks from the lists. Directed activities of this kind should be viewed as preliminary activities to formal handwriting.

1. Writing movements using a paint brush

● Bridges, or hopping, etc.
Clockwise movement - up - over - down. Relaxation exercise: make bridges in the air with wrists and fingers relaxed.
● Waves on the sea or skipping
Relaxation exercise: arms make swaying movements up and down.
● Climbing up and down mountains
Relaxation exercise: with the muscles of the arms, wrists and fingers loose, flap hands up and down.

- Snakes and ladders
  Show children how to fill a page with curves of various colours and sizes.
  Add ladders if desired. Relaxation exercise: with arms hanging loosely
  from the shoulder, let hands and fingers flutter limply.
- Coloured Easter eggs
  Paint eggs of various colours with coloured bands round them. Relaxation
  exercise: with elbows resting on the desk, rotate hands from the wrist.
- Pattern
  Show children how to fill the page with a pattern of ovals and straight lines.
  Relaxation exercise: with fingers loose, pretend to play the piano on the
  surface of the desk.

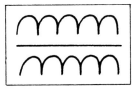 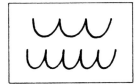 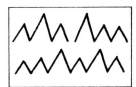

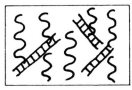 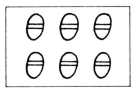 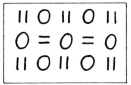

2. Scribbling exercises with a pencil

A pencil with a thick soft lead should be used and the child taught how to
hold it lightly in a reasonably correct manner. The exercises should be done
on sheets of cheap blank paper such as newsprint, and each exercise should
be performed many times. The child should be allowed to scribble freely and
rhythmically to gain confidence and practice in using the new tool correctly.

A relaxation exercise can as usual precede each scribbling exercise.

Exercises such as the following can be devised:

'Smoke from a bonfire'. Draw a small pile of sticks to represent a bonfire and
fill the page with scribbles to represent smoke. The important aspect of the
exercise is how it is performed rather than the quality of the finished product.

In a similar manner pupils may make scribbling lines to represent clouds,
dust billowing from behind a vehicle, waves and spray, a fountain playing,
waterfalls and rapids, a ball bouncing or rolling, a piece of paper blown by
the wind, fireworks, or a wheel turning.

An exercise which will be enjoyed by the children is commonly known as 'taking the pencil for a walk'. The pencil makes a continuous line as in the diagrams below.

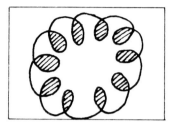 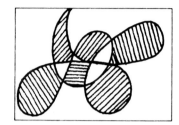

The enclosed spaces can be shaded in with crayons of various colours to make an attractive pattern.

3. Recognising shapes and filling in outlines

Use natural materials such as leaves, together with sensory apparatus such as Montessori insets, wood and cardboard shapes and profiles of trees. Templates for flowers, leaves, animals, letters and numbers which are normally found in infant classrooms can be used with advantage at this stage. Children handle these materials and move a finger round the edge to feel the shape. They are then provided with sheets of cheap paper and pencils, crayons or coloured pencils with which they draw round the shape. The outline thus drawn can then be filled in with coloured pencil. When one outline has been filled in, the children may be allowed to choose other insets and fill their paper or a page of their large writing books with coloured shapes. Children should not be asked to trace round small or intricate shapes, nor should they be allowed to use small stubs of crayon or pencil.

4. Rhythmic writing patterns to music, rhyme or counting

Children who have performed the exercises detailed in the earlier sections should now be beginning to sit correctly when drawing and writing and be better able to use a pencil in a reasonably satisfactory manner. Attention must now be placed increasingly on the ease and rhythm of writing. The following exercises will give pleasure to a child and help to impress the need to move the pencil smoothly and steadily. The teacher must recognise that in the early stages it is more important to observe the writer than it is to pay attention to the end product.

These exercises can be used with advantage at all stages of instruction throughout the school.

● Rhythmic patterns which progress across the page from left to right are performed to the recitation of a nursery rhyme or to counting. The five patterns illustrated at the top of the next page give practice in making all the movements used in writing.

Jack and Jill went up the hill to fetch a pail of water, etc.

Mary, Mary quite contrary, etc.   Humpty Dumpty sat on a wall, etc.

Hickory, Dickory, Dock, etc.   One two, buckle my shoe, etc.

The exercise can also be performed to a steady repetition of *'one, two,'* where the downstroke is made on the count of one and the upstroke on the count of two. If a rhyme is used, each stroke can be associated with a syllable but a very precise metrical correspondence need not be sought. As long as the children say the verse steadily and write fluently and rhythmically as they repeat the words, the purpose of the exercise will be served.

Contents

Page-by-page guide

Lower case letter families 1–4

A1 The twenty-six lower case letters are presented in four families of six or seven. They are intended for observation and discussion, not for writing practice at this stage. They provide an opportunity for teachers to demonstrate the movement common to each family of letters and to emphasise the starting point and direction of movement. They also provide an opportunity to draw attention to the exit hooks on some letters and to point out that these should not be over-emphasised.

- Family 1: *a c d e g o q* are based on an oval, starting at '1 o'clock' and moving anticlockwise.
- Family 2: *b h k m n p r* are based on the bridge pattern, which should not be too wide.
- Family 3: *f i j l t z* are based on vertical and/or horizontal straight lines.
- Family 4: *u* and *y* are based on the swings pattern, which should be compact; *v w x* are based on diagonals, while *s* is a special case with reverse direction curves.

Pattern practice for lower case letter family 1

A2 The balloons are oval, as this is the basic shape for this family. Children start at the dot and move the pencil anticlockwise. The balloons are followed by a more formal exercise: rows of ovals to observe, to trace and finally to write freehand.

A3 The portholes are oval as this is the basic shape for this family. The aeroplane trails and waves should also be made with continuous anticlockwise movements. There is an opportunity for freehand practice.

Lower case letter family 1

A4–10 Discuss the large model letter at the top of the sheet and trace its shape with your finger to emphasise the direction of movement. The labelled drawing gives an opportunity to work on sound/symbol correspondence for each letter. A row of open letters is provided for practice within a framework and the children then trace, and write freehand, rows of examples of the letter. The exercise at the foot of each page provides a further opportunity for work on sound/symbol correspondence and for practising the new letter as well as any letters already learned.

Pattern practice for lower case letter family 2

A11 The water jets should be drawn by going over the dotted lines with a continuous left to right movement. This shape provides an introduction to the important 'bridges' pattern.

A12 The curves on the umbrellas provide further 'bridges' practice. Two formal rows of 'bridges' pattern follow.

Lower case letter family 2

A13–19 Discuss the large model letter at the top of the sheet and trace its shape with your finger to emphasise the direction of movement. The labelled drawing gives an opportunity to work on sound/symbol correspondence for each letter. A row of open letters is provided for practice within a framework, and the children then trace, and write freehand, rows of examples of the letter. The exercise at the foot of each page is a test of letter recognition as well as a counting exercise and an opportunity to practise writing the letters already learned.

Pattern practice for lower case letter family 3

A20 Drawing horizontal and vertical lines gives a foundation for writing the letters in this family.

A21 This picture provides further practice in drawing vertical lines.

Lower case letter family 3

A22–27 Discuss the large model letter at the top of the sheet and trace its shape with your finger to emphasise the direction of movement. The labelled drawing gives an opportunity to work on sound/symbol correspondence for each letter. A row of open letters is provided for practice within a framework, and the children then trace, and write freehand, rows of examples of the letter.

The exercise at the foot of each page provides an opportunity for letter recognition and work on sound/symbol correspondence.

Note for A22 and A26

Letters *f* and *t* both require two discrete pencil strokes; all other lower case letters (except for *x*) are made with one continuous movement.

Pattern practice for lower case letter family 4

A28 The pathways provide practice in controlled zigzag patterns related to letters with diagonal strokes.

A29 The scalloped patterns on the stall roofs provide practice in the swings pattern which is related to letters *u* and *y* as well as being the basis of most joins in cursive writing. More formal practice follows at the foot of the sheet.

Lower case letter family 4

A30–35 Discuss the large model letter at the top of the sheet and trace its shape with your finger to emphasise the direction of movement. The labelled drawing gives an opportunity to work on sound/symbol correspondence for each letter. A row of open letters is provided for practice within a framework, and the children then trace, and write freehand, rows of examples of the letter. The exercise at the foot of each page provides a further opportunity for work on sound/symbol correspondence and for practising the new letter as well as any letters already learned.

Note for A34

Letter *x* requires two discrete pencil strokes; all other lower case letters (except *f* and *t*) are made with one continuous movement.

Lower case letter families 1–4

A36–39 For each letter family, the children have an opportunity to revise the relevant pattern and then to write a row of examples of each letter. This allows them to concentrate on one basic movement per sheet.

Figures 1–10

A40–41 Discuss each large model figure and trace its shape with your finger to emphasise the direction of movement. There is an opportunity to relate the figure to the word and to the number of objects in an illustration, followed by tracing and then writing each figure freehand.

Poems

A42–44 The number rhyme '1, 2, buckle my shoe' is an example of continuous writing involving most of the lower case letters and all the figures. The children are provided with the usual guidelines so that they can be encouraged to keep 'x' heights constant with ascenders and descenders in proportion.

A45 A list of toys (non-fiction, non-chronological writing) is provided as a model of the style and as a resource for writing out on a separate piece of paper (see A46). This skill is more complex than writing on the same sheet as the model so children may need guidance. This writing exercise could usefully form the basis for assessment and could be an opportunity for pupils to check their work, spot their own errors and, if necessary, repeat the exercise. [See page 16 for a list of criteria for evaluation.] Children could then make lists of their own toys.

A46 This sheet offers a set of ruled and dotted guidelines to be photocopied for extra practice, and in particular for the exercise on A45.

3 Cursive Copymasters B: The joins

Introduction

These copymasters revise the lower case letters, introduce the capital letters and the four basic joins, and provide practice in context.

Contents

Page-by-page guide

Lower case letter families: patterns

B1–5 The key patterns underlying the four basic letter shapes and the basic join pattern (swings) are revised; the children study the patterns, trace them and then write them independently. Where a 'mirror image' pattern is provided, the result will only look right if the basic patterns are uniformly made.

Note for B5
Draw attention to the last two patterns which rise to 'x' height and ascender height alternately.

Two lower case letters, in their families, are provided on each copymaster.

Lower case letter families revised

B6–18 Discuss each large model letter and trace its shape with your finger to emphasise the direction of movement. The labelled drawing gives an opportunity to work on sound/symbol correspondence for each letter. An open letter is provided to give practice within a framework, and the children then trace, and write freehand, examples of the letter.

Note for B16–B18

s is a special case with reverse direction curves; *u* and *y* are based on the swings pattern and *v*, *w* and *x* are based on diagonals.

Note for B13, B15 and B18
f, *t* and *x* require two pencil strokes.

Capital letter families 1–5

B19–20 The twenty–six upper case letters are presented in five families of five or six. They are intended for observation and discussion, not for writing practice at this stage. They provide an opportunity for teachers to demonstrate the movement common to each family of letters and to emphasise the starting point and direction of movement. There are no exit hooks; capital letters are never joined.

- Family 1: *I J L V W Z*   1 stroke; straight lines
- Family 2: *M N T X Y*   2 strokes; straight lines
- Family 3: *A E F H K*   3 strokes; straight lines
- Family 4: *C G O S U*   1 stroke; curved lines
- Family 5: *B D P Q R*   2 strokes; straight/curved lines

B21–25 Each capital letter family is practised in turn, with introductory pattern practice to establish the shapes.

Comparing unjoined and cursive writing

B26 This is the final copymaster before the joins are taught. The poem should be read and enjoyed as well as being used to compare unjoined and cursive writing. Through discussion children should appreciate that cursive writing is easy to read and to write and that they will be learning to write it in the copymasters to follow. (There is no writing activity for this copymaster.) The practice of displaying captions and wall stories in cursive writing as well as print from an early stage is recommended as it helps children to become familiar and comfortable with cursive writing.

The joins

The fluency and rhythm of the *New Nelson Handwriting* cursive style depend on four types of join (see page 4). There are opportunities to practise the relevant pattern on the copymasters.

Join 1
B27–34 Discuss the large model joins and trace them with your finger to emphasise the movement. It is necessary to demonstrate this physically.

Join 1 is made from the exit hook at the base of one letter to the top of the 'x' height of the next. The joining stroke should be at an angle of about 45° to the horizontal.

Children can then trace examples of this join and try writing them independently. Encourage them to use fluent movements in their attempts.

Join 2
B35–38 Discuss the large model joins and trace them with your finger to emphasise the movement. It is necessary to demonstrate this physically.

Join 2 is made from the exit hook at the base of one letter to the mid-point of the ascender of the next. The joining stroke should be at an angle of about 45° to the horizontal, and should continue to the top of the ascender before the pencil comes down to complete the second letter.

Children can then trace examples of this join and try writing them independently. Encourage them to use fluent movements in their attempts.

Joins 1 and 2

B39–40 Read through the words provided for practising these two joins, and if necessary discuss their meanings and usage before the children write.

Join 3

B41–44 Discuss the large model joins and trace them with your finger to emphasise the movement. It is necessary to demonstrate this physically.

Join 3 is made from the conclusion of a letter which ends at the top of the 'x' height to the beginning of a letter which starts at the top of the 'x' height. Demonstrate that this join is a shallow curve that should keep the letters the same distance apart as in the other joins.

Children can then trace examples of this join and try writing them independently. Encourage them to use fluent movements in their attempts.

Join 4

B45–48 Discuss the large model joins and trace them with your finger to emphasise the movement. It is necessary to demonstrate this physically.

Join 4 is made from the conclusion of a letter which ends at the top of the 'x' height to the top of the ascender of the next letter. The joining stroke should be at an angle of about 45° to the horizontal.

Children can then trace examples of this join and try writing them independently. Encourage them to use fluent movements in their attempts.

Joins 3 and 4

B49–50 Read through the words provided for practising these two joins, and discuss their meanings and usage before the children write. All four joins are practised on these copymasters.

The break letters

B51–53 These sheets teach and practise the 'break letters' (*b g j p q s x y z*). Explain that no join is made *after* any of these letters or *to* letter *z*. Demonstrate how the break is made and a constant space left before the next letter. There are logical reasons for the breaks:

g, j, q and *y* all have descenders and any attempt to join on to the next letter would result in either a doubling of the distance between the two letters or a halving of the angle of the ligature.

b, *p* and *s* all conclude with a curve moving in the opposite direction to that of the writing flow.

x and *z* would both be fundamentally altered in shape by the addition of exit hooks.

The words provided for practice should be read through and their meanings and usage discussed before the children write.

e and s

B54–55 These sheets explore the variations in letters *e* and *s* which are caused by the nature of the join they follow. Explain the variations and demonstrate them to show how they occur quite naturally in the flow of cursive writing, before the children practise writing the examples.

A comparison of unjoined/cursive script

B56 This sheet focuses on learning to write the child's own name cursively. The use of 'Teddy Bear' as a model of unjoined and cursive script is to aid teacher demonstration to a large group. The child's copy has to be personalised by the teacher writing the child's name in both types of script. The child then practises his/her own name in cursive script.
This is a useful sheet for profiling/assessment.

Practice through themed words

B57–60 The words chosen for practice on these sheets involve random joins but they are arranged thematically. The words should be familiar but they should be read through and their meanings discussed before they are written.

Figures 1–10 revised

B61–62 These sheets give practice in writing figures, but any child who is not forming the figures satisfactorily might benefit from Copymasters 40 and 41 in Cursive Copymasters A.
Sheet 61 explores basic addition bonds.
Sheet 62 explores number patterns, using symbols and arrows to help children identify the sequences.

Poems and riddles

B63–66 These sheets provide poems and riddles to copy line by line on the copymaster. Each poem/riddle should be read through and enjoyed before it is written out.

- Some children might be encouraged to memorise a favourite poem and share it with the class.
- A collection of riddles or related poems could be started.
- The children could be introduced to the idea of self-assessment and be asked to look at their writing critically. A list of criteria for assessment is on page 16.

B67–69 These sheets provide longer poems to be written out on a separate piece of paper (see B70). Each poem should be read and enjoyed before it is written out.

B70 This sheet offers a set of rules and dotted guidelines to be photocopied for extra practice, and in particular for the exercises on B67-69.

4 Cursive Copymasters 1: Practising the joins

Introduction

The aim of these copymasters is to consolidate the skills learned in Cursive Copymasters B through concentrated practice of the cursive style. There is a strong emphasis on the link between spelling and writing.

Starting dots, tinted letters and directional arrows are dispensed with but the symbols   and   are still used to guide children. As well as a set of ruled and dotted guidelines, a blank sheet representing conventional lined paper is provided for pupils who are ready to begin writing in this size.

Contents

Page-by-page guide

Pattern practice

1:1–2   The key patterns are revisited to develop control and fluency. The children study the patterns and then make them independently. They need to produce very uniform patterns for the 'mirror images' on 1:2 to work.

Alphabetical order

1:3   The children complete the alphabet by inserting the missing letters, and develop their understanding of sound/symbol correspondence by mapping each animal drawing to the appropriate initial.

1:4–7   The lower case and capital letters are revised, now presented in alphabetical order further to develop children's awareness of this way of organising information. There is no starting dot in Cursive Copymasters 1, and children may need guidance in managing the space in the first few attempts.

Figures 0–9 revised

1:8   The figures are revised. Although no figure has a descender, a full set of guidelines is provided to help children to understand where to place each figure in relation to letters which do have descenders.

The joins revised

1:9–12   Discuss the large example at the top of the page, and encourage the children to practise the swings pattern which is the basis for all the joins. They go on to practise each join in the context of whole words, presented in alphabetical order.

The break letters

1:13   Discuss the large examples at the top of the page and encourage the children to practise the swings pattern. They go on to practise the break letters in the context of whole words, presented in alphabetical order.

e and s

1:14–15   These letters vary in shape according to the nature of the join from the previous letter. Study the large examples with the children and then look at the lists of words to identify the variations of e and s. The children count the total number of each variation and write the totals in the boxes. This encourages them to concentrate on the subtly different letter forms before writing the examples.

Writing practice through spelling

These sheets explore spelling while practising handwriting because it is generally accepted that there is a clear link between good spelling and consistent legible writing. There are many other strategies for spelling that can be used alongside the copymasters including:

● teaching the four-step approach: Look, cover, write, check
● discussing the ways in which letter strings represent sounds
● discussing the spelling of words of current common interest
● teaching some key spelling rules
● teaching spellings of some common words and encouraging children to relate these to new words they want to write
● encouraging children to notice exceptions
● teaching children about roots and derivations

Magic e

1:16-20 Discuss the illustrated examples. Discuss and read aloud the pairs of words before they are written in the spaces below; this will help the children to understand how the *e* modifies the vowel sound.

The children could be asked to think of more pairs, or to use a pair of words in a sentence: *'I hate the hat you are wearing.'*

Consonant blends and digraphs

1:21–23 These explore double consonant blends. Look at the illustrated example and point out the underlined double consonant blends. Read and discuss each phrase, sentence or word and ask children to identify the double consonants before writing out the examples.

Lead the group in trying to find more words and phrases containing double consonant blends.

1:24–26 These explore consonant digraphs. Look at the illustrated example and point out the underlined consonant digraphs. Read and discuss the phrases and words before they are written. Ask children to identify the digraphs.

Children could find more words and phrases containing consonant digraphs.

1:27–29 These explore triple consonant blends through phrases and words. Look at the illustrated example and point out the underlined consonant blends. Read and discuss the phrases and words, highlighting the blends, before the children write.

Children could think of more words and phrases containing triple consonant blends.

1:30–31 These explore double consonants. Look at the illustrated examples and point out the underlined double consonants. Read and discuss the words before children write.

Challenge children, working in pairs, to list as many words as possible containing a specified double consonant in a given time.

Vowel sounds

1:32–42 These provide lists of words which cover the equivalent spellings for each vowel sound. Read and discuss the words and illustrations at the top of the page, drawing attention to the different spellings. Read through the words on the page before the children write.

Children could list further examples of each spelling.

Thematically grouped words	Read and discuss these thematically grouped words before the children write them. As the words are selected thematically, spelling patterns are random and the 'look, cover, write, check' approach is appropriate.

1:43   (the body) Children could draw an outline of a body and label the parts appropriately.

1:44   (colours) Children could think of a noun to accompany each colour and make an adjective/noun list:
'blue sky/green grass'

1:45–52   (words for stories) Children might select words from one of the copymasters and weave a story around them. Alternatively, these copymasters could be a resource for spelling when children are writing stories.

Verbs

1:53   Read and discuss the present participles ('*ing*' words) before the children write. Discuss the concept of 'doing' words (verbs).

Ask the children to think of other verbs.

Silent letters

1:54   Read and discuss the statement at the top of the page. Read and discuss the sentences, asking the children to identify the letter(s) not pronounced. Discuss the importance of clear enunciation. Ask the children to write the sentences, underlining the silent letters.

Ask children to collect other examples.

Opposites

1:55   Study and discuss the illustrated words at the top of the page. Read and discuss the pairs of opposites which follow before the children write them. Ask the children to select pairs of opposites from the printed list and write them on the lines below. Two pairs should fit on each line.

Collect further examples.

Contractions

1:56   Read and discuss the statement at the top of the page. Read and discuss the pairs of contractions and full words and discuss pronunciation before the children write the examples.

Ask the children to collect examples of contractions in the course of their reading.

Book titles

1:57–58   Read and discuss the book titles and allow time for children to share memories and opinions of the books. Discuss the two forms of script: upper/lower case cursive and unjoined capitals. Children then write out each title in both forms.

Children could list other popular book titles, and try copying the script on the book jacket to gain an appreciation of different styles for different purposes.

Poetry and prose models

1:59   Read and discuss the rhyme 'Good, better, best'. Discuss the illustrations of good writing posture and emphasise the connection between good posture and good writing. Let the children write the rhyme on a separate sheet (see 1:69). They then look closely at their writing to check the quality. Read the list on page 16 so that the children have criteria for self-assessment. If they are not satisfied with their writing, suggest they try again.

Repeat the process for 'A big turtle'.

1:60–62   Read and discuss the poem. Ask the children to write it out on a separate piece of paper (see 1:69) and perhaps to check their writing as recommended for Copymaster 1:59. Reminders of the criteria will be needed.

1:63–65   Read and discuss the non-fiction text (prose, note form or recipe). Children should understand that handwriting skills are transferred to many different forms of writing, and that these non-fiction texts have a specific function. Try the recipe, for example! After writing it out on a separate piece of paper (see 1:69) the children should carry out self-assessment using the written criteria on 1:63. In discussion, the need to write quickly but still legibly for some purposes and very carefully for others should be highlighted.

1:66–68   Read and discuss the poem and prose extracts. These are considerably longer than previous ones but the pupils working on these copymasters should be able to write on conventional lines with a little guidance (see 1:70). When the writing is finished the children should check the quality. Self-assessment will become automatic if this is regularly practised. The children can also be introduced to the idea of assessing each other's work.

1:69   This sheet offers a set of ruled and dotted guidelines to be photocopied for extra practice, and in particular for the exercises on 1:59–65.

1:70   This sheet represents conventional lined paper and may be copied for extra practice and in particular for the exercises on 1:66–68.

Glossary of terms

Anticlockwise: Moving in a curve from right to left in the opposite direction to the rotation of the hands of a clock.

Assessment: To observe children's writing with a view to determining the effectiveness of the teaching policy.

Ascender: The part of a letter which extends above the height of the other 'ordinary' or 'x' height letters. The letters with ascenders are *b, d, f, h, k, l* and *t*.

Basic (first) join: The curved rising diagonal (45°) ligature which is the most common join in the *New Nelson Handwriting* style.

Break letters: Those nine letters after which a join is not made, *b, g, j, p, q, s, x, y* and *z* in the *New Nelson Handwriting* style.

Bridges pattern: A rhythmically produced sequence of arches from left to right.

Capital letters: The forms of letters used at the beginning of sentences and proper nouns. They are never joined to lower case letters in *New Nelson Handwriting*.

Clockwise: Moving in a curve from left to right, in the manner of the hands of a clock.

Consonant blend: When two or three consonants occur together and the sound associated with the cluster is achievable by blending the individual consonant sounds together e.g. '*brat*', '*scrunch*'.

'c' pattern: The pattern made rhythmically by forming a continuous line of letter *c*s.

$$ccccccccc$$

Cursive: A running hand in which the letters are formed rapidly with a minimum of pen lifts.

Descender: The part of a letter which descends below the base line of the writing. The letters with descenders are *g, j, p, q* and *y*.

Diagonal pattern: The pattern rhythmically formed by joining rising and falling diagonal lines continuously across the page from left to right.

Digraph: When two letters occur together and the sound associated with the pair is not achievable by blending together the individual sounds of the letters e.g. *'chat', 'rein'.*

Fine motor skills: The muscular skills which enable a person to perform controlled and precise movements.

Gross motor skills: The muscular skills which enable a person to perform larger and less co-ordinated movements.

Hook: The small curved line that may be added to some lower case letters where there is a natural tendency to join on to the next letter.

Joined writing: Writing which is cursive in that most of the lower case letters are joined one to another.

Letter families: Groups of lower or upper case letters arranged according to their method of construction.
Ligature: A stroke, either diagonal or horizontal, used to join two letters together. In well-formed handwriting all diagonal ligatures are parallel.
Lower case: The form of letters of the alphabet which are not capital letters. These are sometimes called 'small' but this term is illogical.

Parallel (of writing strokes): Running in the same direction and always at the same distance apart.

Readiness: The point in the development of a child where a formal programme of instruction is likely to be fruitful. Programmes are needed to help children reach this point.
Rhythm: Regular and smooth movement characterised by strong and less strong elements with a definite absence of jerkiness.

Self-assessment: Observation of children's writing and writing habits by the children themselves to determine the quality of their learning and the possible need for further practice.
Sets for writing: Groups of lower case letters sorted according to their points of starting or finishing.
Slope of writing: The angle by which the downstrokes in writing vary from the vertical. Any slope should be at an angle of 6°– 8° and never backwards.
Speed of writing: This varies according to purpose; children need to develop an awareness of the need to write at speed enabling the writer to cope with the demands of school and life without sacrificing legibility and pleasant appearance.
Swings pattern: The pattern formed rhythmically by making a continuous line of loops from left to right.

Tripod grip: The relaxed and correct way of supporting a writing implement between the thumb and next two fingers.

Uniformity: In writing – keeping all 'ordinary' letters the same height and width and keeping spaces between letters and words regular.

Vowel modifier: A letter which, when occurring alongside a vowel or vowel digraph, modifies the vowel sound e.g. *'halt'*, *'arch'*.

'x' height: A technical term in the printing and publishing trades. The height of letters which have neither ascenders nor descenders: *a* is an 'x' height letter.

adjectives 34

Index